Travelator

STEVEN WALING was born in Accrington, Lancashire in 1958, and has lived in Manchester since 1980. He won the Smith/Doorstop Pamphlet Competition with his first publication, *Riding Shotgun*, in 1988, and also that year was a prizewinner in the Lancaster Festival Poetry Competition. He has since published four books, including *Calling Myself On The Phone* (Smith/Doorstop).

**Also by Steven Waling**

*Calling Myself on the Phone* (Smith/Doorstop 2003)
*Mee-Mawing* (Tarantula 1997)
*Invisble Mending* (Ure Group Press 1994)
*What the Snow Believes* (Scratch 1992)
*Riding Shotgun* (Smith/Doorstop 1988)

# Travelator

## Steven Waling

CAMBRIDGE

PUBLISHED BY SALT PUBLISHING
PO Box 937, Great Wilbraham, Cambridge PDO CB21 5JX United Kingdom

All rights reserved

© Steven Waling, 2007

The right of Steven Waling to be identified as the
author of this work has been asserted by him in accordance
with Section 77 of the Copyright, Designs and Patents Act 1988.

This book is in copyright. Subject to statutory exception
and to provisions of relevant collective licensing agreements,
no reproduction of any part may take place without the written
permission of Salt Publishing.

First published 2007

Printed and bound in the United Kingdom by Biddles Ltd

Typeset in Swift 9.5 / 13

*This book is sold subject to the conditions that it shall not,
by way of trade or otherwise, be lent, re-sold, hired out,
or otherwise circulated without the publisher's prior consent
in any form of binding or cover other than that in which
it is published and without a similar condition including this
condition being imposed on the subsequent purchaser.*

ISBN 978 1 84471 314 1 hardback

Salt Publishing Ltd gratefully acknowledges
the financial assistance of Arts Council England

1 3 5 7 9 8 6 4 2

# Contents

**PART I TRAVELATOR: RANDOM SONNETS**

| | |
|---|---|
| Eating Paella | 3 |
| My Bed | 4 |
| Harold Wilson | 5 |
| After Sappho: Fragment 31 | 6 |
| For the Weekend | 7 |
| Homeless | 8 |
| Euro '96 | 9 |
| Mother | 10 |
| Bad Cold | 11 |
| Geocentric | 12 |
| Prospects 2 | 13 |
| The Man Who | 15 |
| The All-Purpose Stars | 16 |
| Travelator | 17 |
| On the Town/ Dun Laoghaire | 18 |
| The Raven | 19 |
| Advice Column | 20 |
| Designer Eyewear | 21 |
| After Much Rain | 22 |
| The Call | 23 |
| Air | 24 |

**PART II**

| | |
|---|---|
| Ghosts on the Wall | 26 |
| In Bed | 34 |
| Three Poems About Love | 35 |
| From the Specials Board | 38 |

| | |
|---|---:|
| Ghost | 42 |
| The Pole Star, for | 43 |
| Poem (Abandoned) | 45 |
| In Hitler's Bath | 46 |
| Exile's Lament | 47 |
| Peace Poem | 49 |
| The Blind Postman | 50 |
| Catching the 22 | 51 |
| Every Planet Has a North | 52 |
| The Westerner | 53 |
| The Man with The Blues Guitar | 54 |
| The Prospects | 55 |
| The Crocodile Opens its Mouth | 56 |
| Trade is Increasing | 57 |
| Before | 58 |
| Another Garage Sunday | 59 |
| Gabba Gabba Hey (To Punk Rock) | 60 |
| You Showed Us Your Row of Cups | 61 |
| Pound Shop | 62 |
| Through the White Hole | 63 |
| Triplets | 64 |
| That Summer | 65 |
| Short Dreams in Didsbury | 66 |
| The Eternal | 67 |
| Lazarus | 68 |
| Cod | 69 |
| Temporary Entrance | 70 |
| The Annunciation | 71 |

# Acknowledgements

Poems have previously been published (sometimes in earlier versions) in *Argotist Online*, *Dusie*, *Lamport Court*, *Moosehead X: Future Welcome*, *The North*, *Not in So Many Words*, *nthposition*, *Poetry Nottingham*, *The Rialto*, *Shadowtrain*, *Smiths Knoll*, *Stride Magazine*, *Taste* (UCLAN Press).

Some poems appeared in *Mee-Mawing: Selected Poems* (Tarantual 1996) and other earlier publications.

The writer acknowledges the financial assistance of the Arts Council of England.

I would also like to thank Fran Pridham for editorial assistance and continued support over many years. I'd have got nowhere without the workshops run by Peter Sansom at the Poetry Business.

# Part I
# Travelator: Random Sonnets

"Each tree stands alone in stillness"
                    TED BERRIGAN

## Eating Paella

ten years before in a restaurant
on the Plaça Real with a friend
from my born-again teens
he's reading Krishnamurti

*Lunch Poems* carried round
the Gaudi streets    down the Ramblas
at midnight   I'm 30
attracted by the girl from San Diego

Then who's that it's you and me
at home for a birthday supper
you're saying a rosary
I'm 40 wondering are the last

ten years a mirage    Well
45 heaves round like a train

## My Bed

Dreaming monsters bullied sci-fi girls
I don't know how I passed my exams

This is what this country means   hills
that used to run mills   Mostly I read Asimov
their witchy shadows and fast-moving streams
and don't do homework   They lock up my books

Fold it up put it away   I never did
but you could if you wanted use the headboard
for a table   Once   I ran down a hill on a
farm visit and couldn't stop   I ran down that slope

so fast I scared myself reaching for stars
from under the blankets    witless
I should have been Robert Heinlein
but the ground came up to meet me   Tripped

# Harold Wilson

Then who's that stepping off his plinth
like a man on his way to work
who strode all the way to Huddersfield

My father came back for all the world
like a man out to buy his tobacco
to stuff in his little slot machine

As if he had a purpose in life
 his hair was black as a peppercorn

They're making a film about cops
by the statue of our ex-PM    the theme
from Z-cars in my ears   I stroll past

to write this down   From Eccles he came
his skin was hard though his heart was soft
and ate whatever was put on his plate

## After Sappho: Fragment 31

Shall I jump over fences to impress
when as I start I look in your eyes &

tell myself to button it lad you don't
have to say anything   Just let me be

a penstroke in a sketch by Hokusai
sometimes I could shout at myself

why am I attempting all these grand &
witty remarks when you catch me &

all speaking leaves   Blue as a heron
that stopped me once on a riverbank

the back of my throat like trousers snagged
crossing a fence   Why should I leave

the arms of not saying a word where
everything important drifts just away &

## For the Weekend

Everywhere the same man washes his car
hours stretch indeterminate in the
cul-de-sacs from one galaxy to the next

Long weekends are a wet black hole
where the tree that bears no fruit's cut down
and neighbours in love with themselves
rise unrefreshed at 11 or 12

More at least than these cooked words
for all this effort in the kitchen   A recipe
ought to have something to show for it

Those days I was able to lie abed
tell huge whoppers all night are gone
I thought we'd all be editors someday
not yet wanting to be tied down

## Homeless

He says   No-one I know voted for him
We're in the cocktail bar   He drinks malts
me a glass of Cabernet. He comes from

the Napa Valley but prefers to drink
South African   3 hundred years of growth
His words never finish in his mouth

they pack their bags   leave home
I've not had a bad glass   I tell him
He nods   Tomorrow I'll meet

a mother in her tin shack in Soweto
with the same look in her eyes   Next morning
watch him drag his case to the taxi

to lay his hat in another town   That afternoon
I give her five rand   praise her clean home

## Euro '96

The largest toilet wall in Europe   Happiness
is the first coffee of the morning   Then bang
The post-box stood guard by the blasted van

Cordon off your heart with scene-of-crime tape

Do the weekly shop then home to the news   Later
no-one died   The sky was Yves Klein blue   It's OK
if I were to blow up anywhere it would be

Make the world a safe place for shopping

Where is that   I was going to get a haircut
but I think I'll wait till I know the score

Let's stand round barriers refusing to move on

Am I the only one didn't hear the bang   Bandaged
Heads   Did us all a favour   That morning I was
in a supermarket   My how we've scrubbed up since

## Mother

The angel on the edge of my bed
smells of patchouli   stands six feet tall.
In all our portraits   I look upward
his light in my eyes   I'm feeling unwell
my stomach churned up   I almost ran out
into the streets to get away   Now bells
ring when they say my name   What's that about

I don't want to know   He said we were to give
a great gift to the world   then locks me straight
in the eye   Dares me   They'd have me live
the rest of my days in blue   His hair was curled
like yours   Look at you now   You'd not believe
what I've sacrificed   A slip of a girl
on a mission   Boy   you give me such trouble

## Bad Cold

The next stop is Besse's o' th' Barn
or a sneeze dismantling the universe
Is that a break in the clouds
next Friday   Nostalgia sets in at 50
I feel every week of my age
Some sweet green tea and a tissue

I need an injection of sun
Because I'm a man it's my job
I'm taking this illness too far
What's that mobbing the lampposts

The sky's an ache   Pigeons
Metaphysical with snot
I sit by the window at the front
my head needs truth   and Nurofen

## Geocentric

Locked out daily   pockets full of coins for the slots
where does the sun sleep when it slopes off at night

One slice of bacon tomato and a rubber egg
does he eat his lunch off the world's flat plate

Still the forecast rain is holding off but do you
fall into space when you reach the horizon

Weather talk round the breakfast room   lashings of
where do you fall to when you're over the edge

toast and porridge the consistency of warm mud
Is the world really a flat as this town   full of

kiss-me-quick gulls and the skrike of salt
will we swim out too far then drop out of sight

The penny arcades have opened their doors
do the lights in the sky revolve around me

# Prospects 2

1.

the prospect of being set free
when the sky is Yves Klein Blue

& I watch the Milky Way
if I crane my neck back far enough

through the rear windows of the car
it rained earlier an owl flew past

& for one second my tongue
becomes familiar with yours exploring

uncertainty
you closed your eyes

an injection of sun these small islands of
snogging in bus-stops at midnight

where the mind spreads out its fear
each tree   in stillness   stands alone

2.

on the horizon of the first time
the moon skulks round banks of cloud

tomorrow my dreams hold rarities
a Fender Les Paul naked on the cover

of my first LP things stop being themselves
turn into ships making landfall

on that blessed isle my hand a page
am I busy ruining sonnets

stars at night I'll reel off reams
under the shadow of this prayer

as hovering it catches the wind
on this bare headland out in the ocean

& everything's supposed to be deep
for now leave me shallow and asleep

## The Man Who

swam through shoals of redundancy
was writing his book on cashless
economy   reinventing Monopoly
without winners of losers   I

never saw him cry   whose idea
of happiness an engine that ran
silk smooth never showed more
than an arm round the wife at

funerals   oblique comments when
I got my BA spoke volumes to
Skodas   imagine him making a film
with pals from the Camera Club who

hid in his workroom from *Neighbours*
on his death bed saying   *I love*

## The All-Purpose Stars

Someone's behaviour is bothering
a significant other   Try not to rescue
everyone today   It's a day for keeping
You might be in a silly mood but

it feels like you're stuck in quicksand
A good day for haircuts    kicking arse
if you're feeling stuck with some ache
you need to tiptoe like a fairy round

Someone in your life has a bee in their bonnet
where what's not in the open
is the tendency to blurt strange truths
at the wrong moment   The way through

is to think about the future beyond
Something hidden will pop out   Careful

## Travelator

Will passengers have their boarding cards ready

Changes of clothes    books    pen in my pocket
the quandaries    No Sharps Allowed    Suitcase
packed    we enter a new country singing
If tears were a staircase

Does this pavement move on forever

I'm a man it's my job to be wrong    Love ends
The sky is Yves Klein Blue    at the terminal I'm
lost in the map of veins    Last Chance to Buy
We'll take our coffee in the American Cafe

Then we fold it all up and put it away

To my heart    girl    you give me such trouble
stepping on a moving pavement on a mission
to depart    I carry *Lunch Poems* round

## On the Town/ Dun Laoghaire

In the harbour no gantries no cranes no
dockers oiled with trade watch buoys bob
on the sceptical sea and the rain moving
toward us   No *I feel like I'm not out of bed yet*

as we wait to walk through the terminal
A pilot boat makes small announcements
to the shore   The Wicklow Hills and twin
power plant chimneys the tallest structures

as we enter a new country singing with
a good exchange rate    Weather fine
and the little white fishing ports gleam
We are not about to change our names
to something easier to pronounce    Someone
nevertheless plays *The Leaving of Liverpool*

# The Raven

All the pets' corners are closed
life too expensive to maintain
the sun bounces off the boating-lake

but the raven the raven
knew the name of a pot-bellied pig
and croaked as we passed:

Love ends   to the pigeons and goats
floating trolleys   MacDonald's cartons
No-one gets the benefit. Peacocks

the chicks in the hatchery   Nothing
in its cage like a poem from childhood
take away nothing equals loss

fold it up and put it away   Nothing
goes anywhere for the next ten years

## Advice Column

*How do I approach a rock star*   You're perkier
which is something   The litany of dubious years
as fly-on-the-wall will go away   *Anyway*

*enough about me*   Take a look at the hassles
in your life   Any caves you can retreat to
Those closest to you are still in a tricky mood

Don't let it get you down   *Madness is doing
the same old things*   Since he stopped drinking
nothing about it seems funny except the way
you're looking at things   Poetry *should* contain
coffee and croissants   Fold it up   put it away

right now you're given different results   Anything
is sortable   eating too few veggies   not wanting
to be tied down   *There are times we need to observe*

## Designer Eyewear

It fills your pockets with rain   Trees and grass
all I recall of the road into Dawlish   Sometimes

We drove South in the old Skoda that kept
breaking down   Sometimes the day's so heavy

And a bridge from then to now includes Dad
blind on half a scrumpy   Nostalgia sets   concrete

Amazing happiness of the first coffee   Don't
let it get you down   We've not been back

Lovely cool evening with the lights coming on
I think of the fires my father lit   A long trip

Perhaps a brass band parping at the front
*Alexander's Ragtime Band*   Or was it Barcelona

The man with a withered arm begging coins
of a currency I can't count   It's the most

## After Much Rain

groans of slow traffic   I don't know anyone
A loud shirt   the night's imitation of day
Watch the cats' eyes blink

as clouds swim in my head like alcohol
move inland threatening worse   Beetles
pick up passengers   head for the suburbs

Enter the pub wearing cash and a smile
scraps of weather talk floating on air

anything is sortable in the back of a cab
in empty space   A man worshipped by rain
heads home   colour drained the cars bare

sharpened headlamps   Something's not said
among the parked-up motors   Shouts of abuse
shut shop windows   A bus sloughs through puddles

# The Call

you know me I always come back bad penny

swear on your mother's you'll look after her
yea I'm coming round now she's distraught

what I'm going to say she'll go ballistic

I'll not let them take me get out soon as
yea darling I'm off to kill some bad men

go off on one look after her promise she'll
yea mate later put her on I've something
yea mate I'll give it five minutes to work out
go on swear it we'll go for a few sherbets

when I get back I'm too old for this don't
I'll be alright I know I know I know listen
I've something to say no listen I haven't

nothing bad just don't do nothing daft

# Air

then fluttered off to the clouds
that caught the back of my throat
that melody  *te recuerdo Amanda*

no attachments trying to remember
but look years later no strings
I lift into flight a new country singing

like tiny ghosts I'd flap after them
birds flying in and out of the bedroom
thirty years ago they were calling

from the radio's dawn chorus
words misremembered misheard
from the upper atmosphere

snatches of song floating down
sometimes I still hear the voices

# Part II

"Do operating witches sit to the left of the ink"

# Ghosts on the Wall

*"I can remember the shocks suffered by small children when they found out that at night in their own cots and under their mothers' eyes their own heads were haunted."*

EVA SVANKMAJEROVA

### 1. MY NAME IS PAVEL

The plane let me in. I'm happiness
counting coins in the hostel
looking for things to amaze me.
Little nudes, fountains. A family
of Roma sell peaches by the tram stop:

buy two for ten crowns, mumble thanks
in very bad English. "There are no beggars,"
(the darkest hair, the darkest eyes)
say the couple from Dorset. "My name
is Pavel," say the bollards by St Nicholas

and there's so many things I'd like;
later in the jazz club, I could kill
for that black leather coat: *My Favourite
Things*. I buy stamps, milk, bread and salami
for breakfast. Oh God, teach me how

(to cross the Charles Bridge arm in arm)
I should sit on the doorstep and wait.

## 2. THE GLOBE BOOKSHOP & CAFE, PRAGUE (SEPT 2004)

Sitting here with a coffee
listening to the buzz of American
and Czech, surrounded by books

One afternoon someone knocked
on the door. We went to open it
and there stood two girls

Today I'm not talking
to anyone, wandering
into a bear's cave
where lunch costs
215 crowns 3 courses
but I don't have to eat

One asked if the Mirgová
family lived here

But right now the sun
floats through the door
reads e-mail the *Prague Post*
decides on the borscht

Mom asked what was wrong
and the girl said that her name
was Zanetta Mirgová

Everything's a warm
contented brown while
outside Prague stirs
like a coffee-cup
under the foamer

We were all astonished
Mom fainted when she heard
it was her little girl

and in my head last night's
jazz band plays a long slow
blues over and over

Alternate verses: Helena Cajokovska, age 14, Prague Remedial School (from
*Romano Suno: Writings & Art work by Romany Children*, Nová kola 2001)

## 3. FREE PHILOSOPHY LECTURE

The blind opera singers of the Karluv Most
and me caught without change. Yesterday
I narrowly avoided getting mugged
by a man in a light blue shirt. Listen:

all people have their own language.
Now I'm sitting upstairs in the Globe;
and there's no words more beautiful than ours
discussing 'the will to change'. I see

a yellow sun that smiles on the world
but Dave from Iowa misses the point,
gets off at the wrong conjunction pursuing
some axiom all his own. Listen: stories

pour like water down these old town walls.
Last night I read poetry in the Tulip,
tonight there's something wrong in the world
but now's not the time, so everyone tells me

the most common risk is pickpockets

as we head for the *Marquis de Sade*.

4. GORGE CROSS BY A BRIDGE

I don't remember dreams but lately
they've involved architecture, striding
streets of Prague in a dazzle of steel
off the river. The same voice announces
stops for the trams and the Metro.

Half-open eyes of buildings follow me.
Do they want me to enter? I stay outside.
Walking through fog to my sister's I found
myself in a field of stones, like the one
they used for the planets in Dr. Who.

But no-one will chase me into winter
while St Vitus broods crabwise on his hill.
My brother and I are like two sparrows,
he has his nest and I have my stories.
I walk past soviet blocks to the pink walls

of the old city. Of course it wasn't bombed.
I took a week away from myself - ach mamo
mamo, kaj tu salas?* found myself running
non-stop downhill when I was eight and
a tree root tripped me. Don't wait for time

to give you her hand. Go out, find
a name for yourself: I call myself home.
My name means Gorge crossed by a bridge.


Oh mother mother, where are you? (Rommani)

## 5. GHOSTS ON THE WALLS

Sometimes I would like to be in the rain.
I gorged on your sculpture all week;
where's the House of the Black Madonna?

Antonín Slavíček, painter of Prague,
couldn't hold a brush after the stroke,
took a gun to his head. No rain all week

but Two Men Pissing, your best work,
round the corner from Charles Bridge.
I've a hollow feeling from not speaking.

Look: all these quaint yellow buildings,
(here is someone who only wants)
a feast of art on the island of Kampa.

## In Bed

Light pollution through the blinds
from the roundabout's floodlights.
The duvet's not big enough
for two and there's your hip which
is always in the wrong position. 2 a.m.
and the traffic never quite stops and
that way's just not comfortable
in a single. We talk, carry each other's
troubles like luggage packed tightly
with pyjamas on top for when it's cold
you're ill, dozing, look at you, sweating.
And if it was so good on that side,
why can't we do it on this? What did
your last servant die of? Sex
apparently—*oooh oh Afternoon Delight*.
I've counted the cranes from your window
and there's eight, brought juice, pills,
slept on the right side, which is the left.
Outside is a scene from a car chase ,
only with more of that please,
whatever it was you were doing
with your hand. Woman in bed, man
attendant; half past early: the party
has only just started and we really
must sleep: tomorrow over desks,
on trains, memories melt into one
hot pool of flesh looking out at
vapour trails and traffic, your car
in the car-park, purring.

# Three Poems About Love

YOU WERE STILL ASLEEP

as light came in through the curtains.
The first bus crawled up the hill. I made this
from a dream of my childhood.

This is the house on the corner. Bought
by an absentee landlord, kept empty
for when the price goes up.
Not in this town. The garage next door

was arsoned. Mum lives up the hill now,
I don't like going back. Nostalgia's
a type of arthritis for the poor
who live in the present. The future's

a new block of flats in Manchester at
a hundred grand a room. C-cold. Blinds
at the window and the traffic at the roundabout
never stops. You were still asleep and I

had the horn for you.

## WHEN YOU LIVED AT THE TOP OF THE HILL

we could see right over the valley,
the fields shining bright in the sun
of your constituency. I sketched

the view, that stand of trees
in the garden where we lay on a blanket
away from the gaze of the voters.

But it wasn't your home and you never felt
more than a guest at the party.
This is the desk you worked at:

piled high with papers, diary for appointments.
Always efficient, me able to look after myself
and bring you tea. Our affair

was sorting itself into friendship
the way a job gets put on the done pile.

GORGEOUS,

that is, drop dead in your jeans
or that top, your eyes so blue
I could learn to swim in them. Look:

I'm doing the butterfly in your iris
and you still make me flutter
though we never quite made it.
Let's hold hands, walk
in these beautiful hills. There are

hills and vales my fingers have mapped
in that body you keep trim
and your hair so blond it shimmers
like a wheatfield. Nevermore:
the sun a glass of wine at evening,
light through the windows and the thought

of the first time I saw you, foot
on a footstool and eyes
so full of alone.

# From the Specials Board

Two girls table 1
baked spuds, tuna mayo,
plot their lives in holiday snaps

    Daydream believer
sweltering in August
the Mamas and Papas

    bring my favourite spaghetti
the Drifters *Up On The Roof*
I think of you on the plane

twist the fork eat wipe
bolognaise off my chin
    tomorrow
when you're over
the jet-lag I'll see you

∼

      Table 2: someone's Gran
drinks tea same time each day
runs through the secrets
she'll never tell

      We sit saying nothing
over coffee cream tea crêpe
al pollo, you read my magazine
I do the crossword

we write together, quiet
as the pen on the page
you're telling me, constant
exhaustion, the world
on your back, all the

troubles in your heart, I want
to reach across
this table-cloth grab
the nothing coming
between

∼

      For the couple
on table 3 two cappuccinos,
a shared pastry and a delicate
plaiting of fingers
      After the ninth
the tenth cup is free; sit for awhile
upstairs no smoking, doodle
in the leather chair. 8 a.m.
air clean as a cough and a verse
I can't get straight

I'd like to stop six months
start again when the sun
batters on the windowpane
thoughts pile up

Pain au chocolat croissant
up a belt notch no will-power
sometimes I'd be happiest
with amnesia. The Metro
slides in and out, with me
on the next

~

Waiting at the counter



(place your orders)




                in chef's whites

## Ghost

Open the door   trip over the cat who isn't
What would you like? Some toast? The past
under foot like some sly creature who enters
but you aren't the English Breakfast type

are you   Anyway, that Christmas you
took me shopping; or the time we sat
then my return          asleep on the pillow
there's still some ghosts I can't get rid of

how long must I look to my heart which
craves attention   food in bowls at regular
intervals? No more, little ghost, will you scratch
at my                    in Lancaster kissing

in the Meeting House      later in Starbucks
when I can't be funny or brave   I'm lying
to say I don't miss midnights watching you
comb your hair   dash to the car   Sometimes

it's hard nurturing the grace of sleeping on beds
couches   the cushion the    took ownership of
you never stayed         through the window
with her own suitcase   porridge or cornflakes?

I could declutter that kitchen    stays ten years
"Dead cat poems. Don't like them. Never have.
But when the buggers die..."*
wherever they go they don't


\* copland smith, *Sarah*

## The Pole Star, for

instance: does morning lift the shutters
off the sun, filter weary light through curtains
as the ghost of bacon and Player's No. 10
bangs the door shut behind him and . . .

    . . . something something something
as the traffic builds up around the same island
it was stuck at last week. I've got money
in my pocket, the new copy of *The North*,

and was once a cog in the wheel
of a genuine miracle, when a coach
I was travelling on ran over a tyre
and refused to turn over. Would you

wait for the bus that growls uphill
and drops the night shift at the corner
as Dad walks to work and I get out of bed?
They slope off to rumours of sleep

and their garages full of old cars
needing oil, new pistons, a bit o' dinner
as we stare at this juggernaut wheel
on the route from Calais to Paris, So

the two-hour stop-over's out of the question?
That year, there's a plague of crickets
in the South of France and I'm walking
with a torch at midnight and the Plough

spotted above while thinking of Dad who said,
"Women don't really like sex." God chased me
as far as Taize where an Irsn Dominican
told me the one where Jesus on his cross

says to Peter, "I've something to show you,"
and Peter runs, finds a ladder, climbs up
to hear wise words from his Saviour:
"I can see your house from up here."

## Poem (Abandoned)

Weeds between sleepers, abandoned.
Wind insinuating, abandoned, through
the bricked-up abandoned windows
in the stationmaster's head. Abandoned.

The tea urn can't stop whistling,
abandoned, and passengers abandoned
on platforms are not about to step
through carriage doors, abandoned.

Paperbacks locked in the Waiting Room
(Ladies), abandoned at Page 52,
with the kiss and the handshake
abandoned on the slatted wooden seats.

And the diesel engine stationary,
its journey curtailed, and its driver
shunted to a branch line to the east;
and here's the stationmaster's cap,

abandoned: the wrong place to start from.

# In Hitler's Bath
*(to Lee Miller)*

Why so obsessed with the 2nd World War?
She's scrubbing the eyes off her skin.
If you introduce Hitler into argument
you've already lost: go down that route
we'll end up with the Third Reich.

An SS guard floats down the canal,
male Ophelia in leather coat to die for.
She dares me, pokes her head over the tiles
like a flower in a pot. Documentary
not art, the marvellous in everyone's grasp.

Though she never got the scoop, still,
the burgomeister's daughter, suicided,
plays a mean Pietà of the Couch.
War's a sin except on celluloid,
Saturday afternoons instead of sport:

the way she stares at the camera
as she rinses her perfect skin, her eye
slicing mens' hearts up like bread.

# Exile's Lament

### 1

Mahogany. We brought this with us, along with a clock that broke. Really, our lives do break into little stories that mean things. There's a plate of half-eaten bread and cheese still not stale. We ate

### 2

It's long since the sight of so much blood made any impact on my oseophagus. They'd break our fingers if they caught us singing. I'm afraid I can't recall the words. They mean things, stories. It went something like

### 3

There must be a song but I can't recall one. The door's open and the light's on. Better than the current crop of anecdotal crap. But this table. Everything's left exactly as abandoned by a family at lunch

### 4

shattered. There's these gashes in the sofa, a rake of wounds but no blood. But there ought to be songs. Not that I was ever musical: a voice like chalk on a blackboard. We're trying to make sense of

### 5

our last meal off this, before leaving. A chair knocked over. I also brought back the strong smell of nostalgia in a pouch of tobacco. I once tried riding a bike. But that's gone, smoked years ago. Look, the windows

6

They missed. I wasn't much cop but if I'd persisted we'd be cycling home. There was one song. But when we walk through to the back room, we see them. "Exiles' Lament", "Homeland Dear Homeland," something like

## Peace Poem

Sometimes you have to put on noise
to acheive a bit of peace, like now
when I play my Hildegaard of Bingen
to clear the mind. Or turn off the news,

put on a punk rock compilation
because the kids who rule the world
are playing with their toys again.
High voices sing the love of Christ

like a salve or balm, then I pick
at the scab of frustration with some
furious guitar. Which is better?
I don't know: but when a hole opens

in my prayer life and I'm morose
as a rainstorm at the zoo
my thoughts rumble like traffic
stuck at the lights. So:

Dame Hildegaard today: heaven
attached to the earth by a thread.

# The Blind Postman

We know you too well, Mr Mailbags,
your white stick tapping the ground,
your bag of midnight messages,

bills and official letters, catalogues
of erotic underwear and biros
stuffed in charity envelopes.

Sometimes, we good citizens dream
of stealing your sack, and the bike
tied to its post on the corner,

slipping letters with faint odours
of *Roses of Picardy* through doors
on foreign culs-de-sac or the Close

you always missed where someone
even now waits patiently at home
for the stroke of someone's signature.

## Catching the 22
i.m. *Kenneth Koch*

'So many writers, it seems, are after the poetry of everyday life.
Unfortunately, the average poet's thoughts are about as boring as a reality
TV show, only more pretentious. (Bus-stop epiphanies and walks in the park
abound.)'
                                                                    JANE YEH

Street furniture becomes ridiculous:
performing for cameras at junctions;
and in this neck of the suburbs the poets
stack themselves up in wet shelters
like the famous Morecombe joke.
His face got stuck in this grin
after waiting for hours in the wind
for something that never turned up.

Reading your books was three buses
arriving at once. Always the same:
he waits years for a chance of escape;
when three arrive at once he can't decide
which one gets him home. You wrote
'Best Wishes' in his copy of *One Train*,
talked Appollinaire in the Pizza Express.

When his bus finally turns up,
the driver is crying his eyes out.
'I've been driving in circles for years,'
he says, 'trying to figure this final verse,
and here you are, my very last fare.'

## Every Planet Has a North

Half the year's darker than matter
between galaxies and nobody calls
but the old still speak of that star,
his tinfoil suit, the dawn they woke
to rain and their futures migrated.

Where the last speakers of Guttural
keen to stormtunes each evening
that enter your brain like drizzle:
acid drips for days, and numbs
all thought of departure.

The monorails no longer run here
girls in short silver skirts
don't dance with green-skinned boys
in a blue moon's halls, and no-one
asks what crime they've committed.

Each night the Pro-Consul reports
"nothing happened" in an Empire
that fell long before he was born,
and dreams of prodigal daughters
returning with light in their hair.

# The Westerner

Of course he's not set foot there
but carries his map of the Old West
inscribed on the back of his heart.
He knows each mesa in California,
each chimney in Monument Valley.

His parents, he says, conceived him
in a motel bedroom in Vegas
where there were Indians in the bars
like the ones printed on the walls
of the Saddles Amusement Arcade

on Central Pier. "I put all my feelings
about my friends death from cancer
in that chapter with the massacre
where he rides all night with a hole
in his side the size of Kansas

but still can't save his bride. Poetry
or the nearest I'll get." He blames
the state of the world on the lack
of a new album from Steely Dan
and plays me *The Best of the Eagles*.

## The Man with The Blues Guitar

Who never joined in the washing-up
but paradiddled through his hang-ups
in the room next door? The drummer

with no rhythm. A certain stamp. I nod:
*Handwriting*, you say, *eventually*,
cross-legged, out of Picasso: *it's like* . . .

Buddha descended from Parys Mountain
via Memphis to the Delta Blues. My turn
to wash up, while you slide down

the surface, a chord on the edge
of remembrance: years later, you'll catch
a dose of employment or marriage,

I'll hear your playing pubs round Wylfa
with a band and a riff of Howlin' Wolf's.
I pick up the cups, you pick your guitar,
a joint you don't offer jags from your mouth.

## The Prospects

The prospect of happiness is
an island at the top of the world

and ships that return on the trade winds
with news of a city that drifts on the tides
beyond that point on the compass
where maps scorch into dragon-flames

and sailors fall off the edge
intoning names of places they'd heard of
where the sea blue as the virgin's dress
shines like the crowned heads of Europe.

But when we make landfall at last
with our dreams locked up in the hold

whatever it is we were looking for
on this bare headland out in the ocean
has jumped ship to the next blessed isle
or the next or the next after that.

## The Crocodile Opens its Mouth

so he aims his gun as a warning.
To make conversation, the crocodile
says "Haven't your prospects improved?
Now you can drive into Rosebank,
buy that shirt to wear to funerals."

The man aims at a rock just off
to the left. The crocodile sings:
"The body takes its own housing
wherever it goes." Tail brushing,
he lets small birds floss his teeth.

On the stoep, someone's dreaming
of the five malls of Gabaronne.
He still has his eye on that shirt,
zig-zag patterned black and white
like the back of a zebra. "Look
at what your freedom can buy!"

He wonders whether to shoot
or ride on the kombi to town
to purchase that beautiful silk.

## Trade is Increasing

said the chief, ordering another plate
and a bottle of Castle. The boy walked
free into the darkness. The sun never
knew how wonderful it was:
I love this place. The little priests:

birds skipping along the verge,
past the stalls selling car-parts.
The future welcomes a tour-bus
from Dhaka; here's a photo of his bed.
Remember quiet evenings by the fire

in the days before civilisation?
We gasped at the smoke, told stories
of streets paved with laughter, longed
for the certainty of walls. My guide
shouts at kids as if they were his.

Everyone knows him, shakes his hand
as if he's their closest friend. Once
one of the tribe brought home an Idea.
We threw it on the flames; it cooked.
I'll take the sun on Vilakazi Street,

eating fried chicken with the All-Stars
centre-forward, over what happened
to the boy who carried Hector Peterson
home to his mother. "Delicious,"
I said, leaving room for dessert.

·

# Before

reading aloud from the paper,
that old-fashioned chivalry arm
gentled round her waist - unnatural

and stilted - what are you doing
in leathers standing by the wall
arm-in-arm with someone impossibly

delicate, I and my sisters gleams
of polished chrome as you mount
and she climbs on behind? Who are you?

- there's something about your grin
that decade of Elvis, how does it turn
years on to a slumped idealogue

who looks like but can't be? Eat
your chips from paper, she a sparrow
you hold like she might but won't

when her father dies. Some convoluted
plot - I can't believe you that slim
when you're on your way to the sea

and her - reduced to speechlessness,
gunning the pedal as the bike ignites,
adjusting the strap of your helmet,

roaring streak of Black Lightning,
black hair, black eyes, resolved in a
beautiful satisfying way, the first

of the engines that end up in bits.

## Another Garage Sunday

Time passed staring at grounded rainbows
the sloosh of wheels through puddles
spreading across a bleached forecourt

Down the road a priest says early mass
to two old women and a monk where the air
was always queasy I'd rush to serve them

Not forgotten that stale smell of oil
from the pressed nozzle though mostly
sun rises from behind wet roofs stretches

Into a cramped cabin where I'd watch
silent pumps that stood unreadable unfit
with sick-sweet fuel that flowed yawning

Moaning of traffic and the cost chill air
dissolves in sex at No 36 watch the clocks
spin up the miles yawning yellow arms

Playing Russian roulette tanks full
of obsequious smiles then three cars
arrived at once across the estate bored

Cars in garages wait out for Sunday
runs nothing is about to happen in triggers
soldiers on parade salute their petrol heads

## Gabba Gabba Hey (To Punk Rock)

And I met you again that day in Moss Side
with Dad and the Anti-Nazi League.
Noise annoys: confused between God

and libido, my place in the grand scheme
of hatred and bad taste, I never had the gear,
though in one early photo I'm Joey Ramone.

Thanks: you poured my rage
into a few seven-inch singles, tapes,
a man with a Silvertone guitar.

On the road from New Mills
I first fell in love
crashing down a cataract of spit:

from the boss's car radio
to the storm in my jeans, heart
pinned together

in one almighty sulk. One chord wonders,
a homemade anarchist's bomb
in the year of the Jubilee, boredom sprayed

over crumbling home town walls,
toes pointed in, singing *Alison*,
wearing my National Health specs.

## You Showed Us Your Row of Cups

Remember Wednesday afternoons
when Anxiety always picked us
for his team at football
out in freezing fields lined up
against uniform walls we stood
like the unbuttered face of white bread
when the captains of houses chose sides
and Confidence picked all the bullies
and the lads in smart new kit
as Brilliance and Future Prosperity
chose boys who built guitars
and paid for school meals
while we shivered with the fat boy
who couldn't run in cheap shorts
and pumps off the market
then teamed up with Captain Anxiety
and nobody thought we could win
least of all us and you agreed,
didn't you, with your long corridors
where we waited outside the Head's room
as the games played on without us
and you showed us, didn't you?

# Pound Shop

A cowboy hat that can hold five gallons of
Ramsbottom rain on a wet Friday afternoon in
October 2003

A tartan car blanket that has been to the moon and
warmed the knees of Buzz Aldrin, his security for
the long lunar nights when we weren't allowed to
watch

Magritte's pipe that is not a pipe but a sign or
signifier pointing to something sinister or sexual
occuring at midnight in a Liverpool back street
glimpsed from the car

A CD of traffic on Highway 69 on the evening of the
28th October 1958 as a young Bob Dylan turns on
the radio and hears the fuzz of electricity from a
hospital bed in Accrington

A box of loose stamps from the Island of Doctor
Moreau, depicting its flora, fauna and significant
Landmarks

The memory of that hot Ramblas night with Heidi
and the transvestites

A book of photographs of famous Lancastrians in
8-hole Doc Marten's boots, entitled A Book of
Stamps (foxed, torn, shredded, chewed by the dog)

A plate full of buttered Chorley cakes, recovered
from the tomb of King Rameses III, one day and
three millenia old

## Through the White Hole

This far out, space isn't black it's white.

The woman across from me is reading
as her son the mountaineer
climbs the sheer face of her calm.

Outside the window an abstract hedge,
trees looming. Is that really my face?
It's like the whole country wears
a badly fitting suit and a tie as it

strains through raw cotton to Bristol Temple Meads
and my interview. The lighting of lamps
on fogbound stations breaks my heart,
they offer two A's and a C.

Can I breathe in this atmosphere?
Professors speak like newsreaders
chatting theology. Antique furniture
burnished as the day it was bought

and I don't get the grades. In a galaxy
far far away, a girl in a summer dress
steps onto the platform. My future

slides into the station. I change trains.

## Triplets

Wouldn't it be fine to live
riding back to my roots
left at the traffic lights


The sixties I missed them
out of Liverpool with accents
at this time of the evening


When he steps into the room
it's the kind of day
the music begins


In a voice cracked as
cars on the highway
in the grainy black


We walk its surface
the beat of a dream
of origins going under


If the wind were a colour
like torn-up manuscripts
wear something light

## That Summer

Under a promising moon
I met someone like you on the train.
Who was I that summer?
The journal mentions the summer rain.
Supine under starlight
a white butterfly comes to rest.

It is quite clear what these distinguished:
things, more solid than we are,
as if the light let go along
trees lining this road, now bare.
This is the climactic scene:
he was climbing up the pulpit steps,
Clonk! Oh the excitement—seven, up and alone!
To think that I will never write that year
Time put an arm around my shoulder—
inside the house it was like gold, a pool—
it was not the reality she would have chosen.

## Short Dreams in Didsbury

I stayed one summer in that house
of books on child psychology,
I never disturbed. Two months'
doilies in the dining-room,
cushions and antimacassars.
The past comes in off the street

like someone caught out in the rain.
I'm zipping up my boots, but they all
spoke kind to me. One day I say
something deep to the cat then dawn
and I don't move, my voice invisible
like it's straining through a tea-bag.

The smell of burnt toast, cat food,
and a cough like a stuttering boiler,
dreaming cushions and antimacassars
through one day and into the next
where I wake in the dark on this old
broken bed to snow on the ground.

## The Eternal

swims always around us. Litter
fills the land as diamonds are dug
from deep underground; crushed
detritus of primeval forests

but when I stare at the stars
in the Royal Excange Jewellers
I can't even afford that small one.
Life piles up like an unpaid bill.

I tell myself one day I'll be perfect,
harder than the hardest mineral,
but who am I kidding? Distracted
by the things of this world, I shop.

# Lazarus

He talked in feathery question-marks,
you never got the point of. Nice line
in parlour tricks: I died for real.
I like to think I'm fairly ordinary
but it's like death follows me round.

I tend to do a lot of thinking
but can't remember  much more:
everything is in his voice:
"Come forth!" he boomed
in best stage voice. I stumbled out,

they tell me. Now half the town points:
"Can you tell us a little more
about yourself?" Dogs, parents
of children who died: Mister Miracle
they call me, from one step behind.

How much he must have loved me.
This light is essential to me
because it hurts. I stank of myrhh
tripped over bandages. Don't look at me,
I can't bring them back. How much

the dark keeps creeping underfoot—
though when I'm feeling optimistic
he must have needed me to live—
I'm back there wrapped in quiet,
and every night I wake in sweat.

# Cod

Trawlers drag through Newfoundland seas
deep blacks of the Kingdom of Cod
flow down the throats of our childhood
nations of white fish swimming one creature
the largest amount consumed in living-rooms
in front of *Crackerjack* from last week's Mirror

Waves narrate the legend of icebergs
tea's mashed in the pot dash of sterilised
during Vimto summers of the early 70s
humming *Hot Love* with mushy peas on trays
heaving round the hold slippery with ice
as men in sou'westers steam home

*Salt and vinegar how many chips luv*
*Can do plaice but you'll have to wait*
on their way from Iceland emptying cargo
on the deck at Fleetwood less and less
shoals departed smaller the hunger as deep
eaten with fingers washed down with loss

## Temporary Entrance

                        To be always
available, open all hours like an all-night
garage that sells milk and bread.
But to drive all this way
not to glimpse the coast of France:
though last night's wine conversation
could be said to make up for it.

After several false starts, the day
settles on sunlight, the early
morning walk. Cliffs, beach
and the shut-dowm arcades hibernate—
dormice waiting for changes in the promise
of rain. An indolent temple in the rocks
and a fishing boat

leaving the harbour. This is England
South-East, its language property,
where gales take winter holidays;
while the artists' community of St. Ives
moves by night mysteriously from Cornwall
to this house where breakfast is about
to be served: fruit juice, cereal,
two slices of toast and marmalade.

## The Annunciation

All that holy light gets in your eyes
till you can't tell what's happening
      the angel comes his tidings
resound on air like bells
long after they were tolled

      And when he goes he leaves
a feather in your belly, fear
like a myth embarking on its
long voyage into history
           nine months on
and the dream wakes up bawling
in a mess of muddy straw

as the angel's words
dance on the tip of your tongue
      flames
burning the roof of your mouth